SAN FRANCISCO

A PHOTOGRAPHIC PORTRAIT

Brad Perks

First published in the United States
of America by:

Twin Lights Publishers, Inc.
8 Hale Street
Rockport, Massachusetts 01966
Telephone: (978) 546-7398
http://www.twinlightspub.com

ISBN-13: 978-1-885435-60-6
ISBN-10: 1-885435-60-6

10 9 8 7 6 5 4 3 2 1

Editorial researched and written by
Francesca Yates and Duncan Yates

Book design by
SYP Design & Production, Inc.
http://www.sypdesign.com

Printed in China

INTRODUCTION

In 1847, Yerba Buena, a little town of about a thousand people, changed its name to San Francisco. The new name stuck.

The Mexican-American War changed the name of the city, and the California Gold Rush changed just about everything else. The San Francisco "forty-niners" as they would soon be called, started to arrive. Within a year or two, 100,000 prospectors came to San Francisco from all over the world.

It was, however, the discovery of Nevada's Comstock silver lode that changed San Francisco forever. The California Gold Rush of 1848 had turned San Francisco's banks into the most powerful in the West. Nevada may have mined the silver, but it was San Francisco that banked the 300 million dollars.

On the morning of April 18, 1906, the most discussed earthquake in world history occurred. Official figures said only 500 people died, but 225,000 were left homeless. Ruptured gas mains ignited a city-wide holocaust, while the rest of the city's 400,000 people could do nothing more than watch the city burn from the Oakland hills.

Though the Great Earthquake and Fire of 1906 was a national disaster, it was merely another obstacle for the city that had invented the wild and raucous Barbary Coast. There had been three major earthquakes since 1865, and too many holocausts to count. The city was like some invincible hand-made sword, folding over on itself, again and again, with hammers and fire and time.

San Francisco re-invented itself again after World War II. Now people weren't discovering gold, they were discovering themselves. The beatniks begat the hippies...and the word went around. By 1967, the "Summer of Love," the old Victorian haunts of Haight-Ashbury overflowed with 100,000 Flower Children, the last, great migration of people to San Francisco.

It was six years before the Great Fire of 1906 when the design for the city flag was chosen. The city fathers decided on a field of white, trimmed with gold, and in the middle—a mythical phoenix, rising. This is the city of San Francisco.

Cable Car on Hyde Street

Like a mountain goat, the Hyde Street cable car clings to the tracks at the top of one of San Francisco's world-famous hills. The exciting climb rewards riders with picture postcard views of the Bay, Alcatraz Island, and the headlands beyond.

POWELL
AND
MARKET

12

Meet me
at the
St. Francis

HYDE ∞ BEACH
FISHERMANS
WHARF

Embarcadero and Transamerica Pyramid, Pier 3 *(above)*

The stunning light at sunset almost finds itself in competition with the skyline of San Francisco. This fight happens every night along the Embarcadero.

The San Francisco Skyline from the Berkeley Hills *(opposite)*

An evening drive through the Berkeley Hills is a perfect way to get a sense of the layout of the city and the Bay.

View from the Bridge *(opposite)*

Nestled in a wooded setting ten minutes from the Golden Gate Bridge are the Hi-Marin Headlands of the Golden Gate National Recreational Area, affording breathtaking ocean vistas and trails that lead to scenic beaches with little evidence of human presence.

Skyline from Treasure Island *(above)*

Treasure Island is a 403-acre man-made island, built in San Francisco Bay as the site of the 1939 Golden Gate International Exposition. The world's fair celebrated the completion of the Golden Gate and Bay Bridges and San Francisco's growing prominence in Pacific trade.

Grapes Ripe for Harvesting *(above)*

Napa Valley grapes have been nurtured in a Mediterranean-style climate—dry, sunny and warm—and will be harvested at the moment of perfection. Napa Valley is known for its extraordinary range of wines, from rich reds to spicy zinfandels and creamy chardonnays.

Harvest Time *(above)*

Napa Valley is the largest producer of California wines which, in turn, account for over 90% of wine production in North America. The vintners here have perfected the marketing of the "wine tour" and attract millions of enthusiasts yearly from around the world.

East Bay Farmlands *(previous page)*

The velvety hills of Morgan Territory undulate in lush, green ripples under twilight skies in this pristine East Bay farmland country.

Mount Diablo, East Bay *(above)*

The sun hovers in purple twilight over the craggy peaks of Mount Diablo as if waiting for permission to set.

Vineyard in Napa Valley *(opposite)*

Tilting with windmills in Napa Valley may not be your idea of fun, but, there is a Quixote Winery in the Valley that was started by a local vintner who is famous for his iconoclastic individualism.

Mount Diablo State Park *(top)*

Mount Diablo stands on the edge of California's Great Central Valley. In the late 1800s, you could ride a stagecoach to the 3,849-foot summit. Today the trip to the top is a lot easier and offers spectacular views of the Sierra Nevadas to the East and beyond.

Rainbow over Tilden Park *(opposite)*

Tilden Park offers many ways to enjoy the outdoors—swimming in Lake Anza, hiking, riding on real horses or hand-carved carousel horses, or enjoying a steam train. From October to April, the South Park Drive entrance is closed for the annual salamander migration.

The View from Potrero Hill *(above)*

Potrero Hill is a thriving neighborhood situated on one of San
Francisco's gentler slopes overlooking the Bay. Its claim to fame
is Vermont Street. Lombard Street
claims to be the "crookedest
street" in town, however, Vermont
Street actually is the crookedest!

Lightning Over Lafayette *(above)*

Captured here is the biggest lightning show in the Bay Area in nearly 20 years. Remnants of a tropical storm off of Baja, California created multiple lighting bolts across the sky which continued to pass over the city through the night, creating amazing lights.

**San Francisco Bay at Sunset
from Oakland Hills** *(above)*

Oakland is a city of 400,000 on the
northeast end of the Bay that connects with San Francisco via the
Bay Bridge. The Oakland Hills are
covered offering beautifully land-
scaped homes with stunning views
of San Francisco and the Bay.

Lafayette Reservoir *(above)*

Captured in the purple haze of
sunset, Lafayette Reservoir, in the
East bay area, is an idyllic, quick
getaway for city dwellers. The lake
boasts of great trout fishing, and
the public areas around the
water's edge have hiking trails and
picnicking areas.

Tiburon at Sunrise *(opposite)*

Tiburon is a quaint town at the end of the Tiburon Peninsula that curls out into San Francisco Bay. This early fishing village eventually became an art colony. Here you can shop, dine, and enjoy beautifully restored buildings on historic Main Street and Ark Row.

Sunset from Berkeley Marina *(above)*

A pink glow is all that is left of another beautiful day on San Francisco Bay.

San Francisco Bay From Treasure Island *(above)*

The city looks freshly washed in the gleam of a sunny, new day. The best weather months to visit San Francisco are April, May, September, October and November. December through March is the city's rainy season.

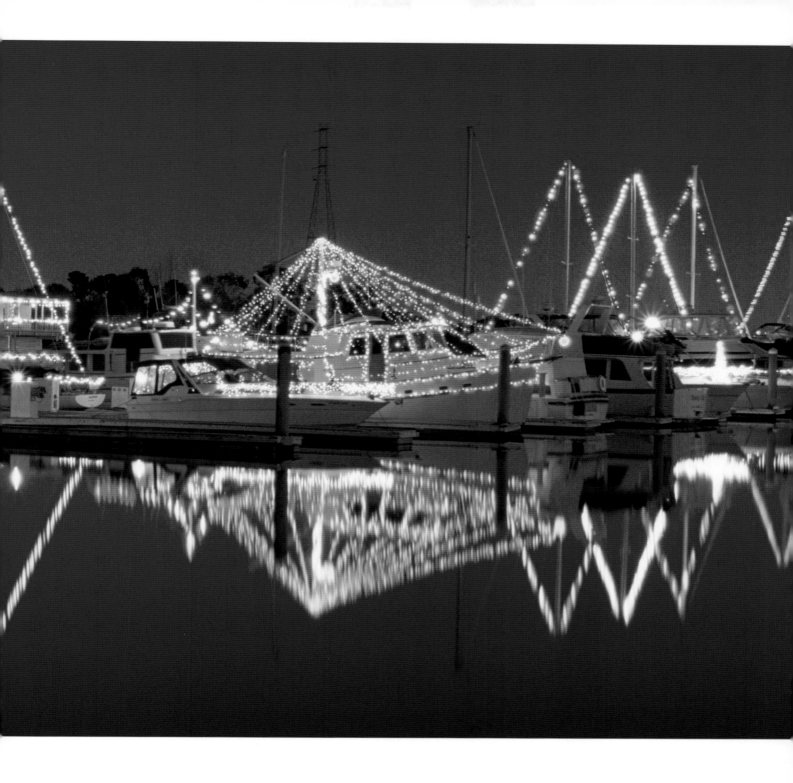

Holiday Lights at Loch Lomand Marina *(above)*

During the holidays in San Francisco, boating enthusiasts show their Christmas spirit by decorating their boats with colorful lights.

Full Moon at Sunrise from the Berkeley Hills *(opposite)*

Shimmering like a French-Impressionist painting, San Francisco hovers in the mist before starting her busy day.

Golden Gate Bridge at Sunset *(above)*

In this beautiful harbor setting, fuel oil is imported and transported in such high volumes that San Francisco has become one of the busiest ports in the country.

Alcatraz Island *(above)*

When Alcatraz Island was discovered by Spanish soldiers in 1775, it became an important defense garrison for the bay. It subsequently became a notorious, maximum security prison nicknamed "The Rock." In 1969, a group called "Indians of All Tribes" occupied the Island for 19 months and declared that they were taking back their land. This single event changed the course of history and fueled the Indian movement around the world.

San Ramon *(above)*

A wealthy, fast-growing suburb in San Francisco's East Bay area 40 minutes from the city, San Ramon and its Tri-Valley neighbors boast of 16 award winning wineries and appropriately dubs itself "California's Original Wine Country."

Corinthian Yacht Club, Tiboron
(above)

Built in 1886 in this scenic cove, the Corinthian Yacht Club is one of California's oldest landmarks. It has been at the forefront of the sailing tradition in the Bay Area, founding such popular traditions as Opening Day on the Bay and The Blessing of the Fleet.

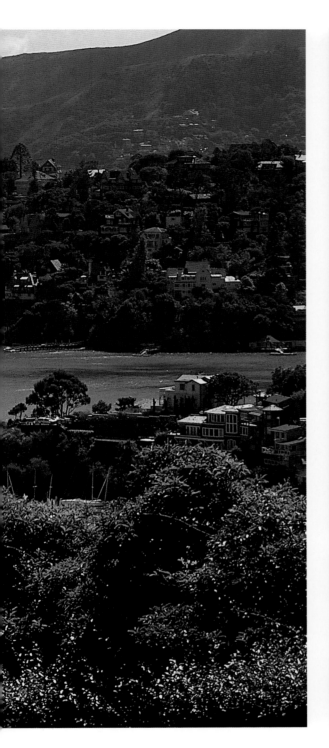

St. Francis Yacht Club *(above)*

For 75 years, this 2,300-member yacht club has become a major player in world-class sailing events. The club is host to over 40 regattas on the Bay. It was the site of the 2000 US Olympic Sailing Trials and continues to host World and National Championships.

Marin Headlands Fog *(previous page)*

The curtain rises slowly in a theater of sky, water and wind. On a summer afternoon, look west from downtown San Francisco up Market Street and watch the fog crawling over Twin Peaks and cascading down the slopes like a grand waterfall in slow motion.

Redwood Regional Park *(opposite)*

After many redwood trees were cut down to build San Francisco and surrounding communities, logging was banned in the park. Today redwoods tower above the ridges, some reaching 100-feet. Former mill sites now serve as picnic areas in the park.

Eucalyptus Trees in Fog *(above)*

Walking among Tilden Park's fragrant eucalyptus trees in the early morning fog, it is hard to believe that these lofty, majestic trees are not native to California. They were brought here by Australian gold seekers who thought the landscape was a bit too barren.

The Bay Trail *(above)*

Hikers along the Bay Trail enjoy
the constant beauty of ever-
changing views of trees, rocky
cliffs and ocean in the Golden Gate
National Recreational Area, one of
the largest national urban parks in
the world.

10 Mile Beach *(above)*

Point Reyes National Seashore is a masterpiece of thundering ocean breakers, open grasslands, and forested ridges. Located just north of San Francisco on the Marin County coast, the park's numerous bays, lagoons and estuaries are popular with paddling enthusiasts.

Sunset over Pacific Ocean (above)

Twenty minutes from San Francisco, Pacifica is flanked by pristine parks and recreational areas to the East and the beautiful Pacific Ocean to the West. This valley town was named in honor of sculptor Ralph Stackpole's 80-ft. statue at the 1939 Golden Gate International Exposition.

Rodeo Beach, Golden Gate Recreational Park (opposite)

There are several wind-swept beaches in the San Francisco area that allow nudity; however, Rodeo Beach is the only nude beach in the Marin Headlands with spectacular frontage on the Pacific Ocean.

Surfing Maverick Waves *(opposite)*

Surfing maverick waves is not for the weak at heart. Every year, the Mavericks Surf Contest gives surfers 24 hours notice to show up at Half Moon Bay and ride some of the biggest, most dangerous waves on earth.

Wind Surfing at Crissy Fields, Golden Gate National Recreation Area *(above)*

Even if you aren't into wind surfing, the walk from Crissy Fields to Fort Point is one of the most beautiful urban walks in the country, with panoramic views of the Bay.

The Bay Trail in Berkeley *(above)*

A lone cyclist enjoys a golden sunset along the Bay Trail. Halfway to completion, the Trail will encircle San Francisco and San Pablo Bays with a continuous 400-mile network of bicycling and hiking trails.

**Fishing in the Bay, Golden Gate
National Recreational Area** *(above)*

Enjoying a solitary moment fishing
in the bay, it would be easy to
believe that the sun was setting
just to entertain you.

Pier 39 at Fisherman's Wharf *(above)*

Fisherman's Wharf is San
Francisco's most popular attraction, full of souvenir shops, restaurants, a Venetian carousel and
unsurpassed views of the "City on
the Bay." The city's best street
performers stop by regularly to
entertain the crowds.

Surfing at Fort Point *(opposite)*

For over 200 years, the waterfront
between the marina and Fort Point
was part of the Presidio. Today it
is reserved for hikers, bikers, and
even surfing fans.

Sailboats at Sunset *(top)*

Sailors reluctantly set their sails toward land at the end of another exhiliarating day on the Bay.

Sunset on San Francisco Bay, from Berkeley Hills *(bottom)*

Well-known for its spectacular sunsets, San Francisco was called "The Sunset City" at the turn of the 19th century.

Downtown San Francisco *(opposite)*

The streets of San Francisco were laid out as if the city planners had simply dropped a normal grid pattern onto the steeply undulating terrain, which resulted in hilly streets that rise and fall like ocean waves.

San Francisco's Financial District (above)

San Francisco's financial district is the fourth largest in the country. Other buildings in the district are playfully reflected here in the wavy façade of the Bank of America skyscraper.

Yerba Buena Gardens (opposite)

Newsweek Magazine calls Yerba Buena Gardens "the most concentrated arts district west of the Hudson River." This successful urban reclamation project includes the San Francisco Museum of Modern Art, Yerba Buena Center for the Arts, and other fine galleries and museums.

Golden Gate National Recreation Area *(above)*

Fog is a constant visitor to the Golden Gate National Recreation Area, the largest urban national park in the world. The park encompasses 28 miles of coastline and is two-and-one-half times the size of San Francisco.

Sunset at Baker Beach *(opposite)*

Mile-long Baker Beach lies at the foot of rugged serpentine cliffs west of the Golden Gate. Large waves, undertow, and rip currents make for dangerous swimming, but the panoramic views of the Golden Gate Bridge, Marin Headlands and Lands End are safe to enjoy!

The Bay Bridge at Sunset *(opposite)*

The San Francisco-Oakland Bay Bridge spans the Bay and connects Oakland to San Francisco. Like the Golden Gate Bridge, which was built simultaneously, the Bay Bridge is an engineering marvel with two major segments that connect a central island, Yerba Buena Island, to each shore.

4th of July Fireworks *(above)*

Independence Day is celebrated with a full day of free entertainment along San Francisco's waterfront, from Ghirardelli Square and Aquatic Park along Fisherman's Wharf, to Pier 39. The day climaxes with a dazzling display of fireworks that can be seen for miles.

Gay Freedom Day Parade, Market Street *(above)*

Founded in 1978, the internationally-known Gay Freedom Day Parade is one of the more popular minority parades in San Francisco.

Mission Street Fair Carnival
(opposite, top)

Think Rio in February, but add a little fog and limit the party to one afternoon only—every Memorial Day weekend.

Bay to Breakers Race
(opposite, bottom)

Bay to Breakers is the oldest, consecutively-run footrace in the world. The 12K race was established in 1912 as a way to boost the spirit of San Francisco after the devastation of the 1906 earthquake.

Gay Freedom Day Parade, Market Street *(above)*

The rainbow flag, now accepted as the universal symbol of the Gay community, first appeared in 1978. It was designed by San Francisco artist, Gilbert Baker.

Street Dancer *(opposite)*

The Mission Street Fair Carnival is San Francisco's answer to Rio's Carnivale, an annual party attended by more than a half million enthusiasts. The warehouse district is transformed into a Latin spectacle with the tropical colors of samba bands, floats, and dancers.

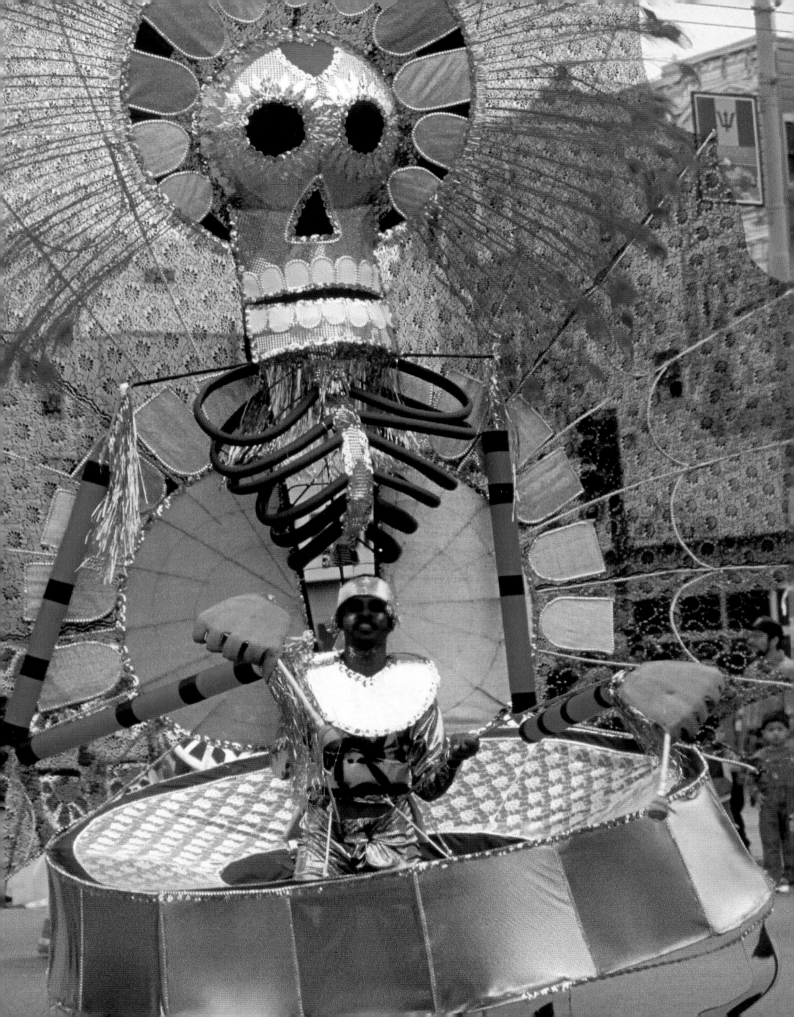

Lincoln Golf Course *(above)*

In this magnificent setting, the oldest and largest continuous event in U.S. golf history is held—the San Francisco City Golf Championship.

Palace of Fine Arts *(opposite)*

This palatial structure was built in 1915 for San Francisco's Panama-Pacific International Exposition. It features a classical Roman rotunda with curved colonnades. Visitors come here to picnic by the lake and visit the Exploratorium's hands-on science exhibits.

The Seven Sisters *(previous page)*

This colorful row of classic Victorian houses, also nicknamed "Postcard Row," is one of the most photographed images in San Francisco and has appeared in countless movies and commercials.

Coit Tower, Telegraph Hill *(opposite)*

Lillie Coit, a colorful and eccentric citizen of San Francisco, bequeathed part of her fortune to her beloved city to beautify Telegraph Hill. Famed architect Arthur Brown's concrete Art-Deco tower was dedicated in 1933 and rises 212 feet above the Hill.

Victorian Mansions, Pacific Heights
(above)

By 1887, many people were beginning to paint their homes in brighter, lighter colors, which became one of the most easily identifiable traits of Victorian architecture.

Sunset District (top)

On an 1853 map, the Sunset District was aptly called "The Great Sand Bank." Embracing most of the city west of Twin Peaks and south of Golden Gate Park, it remained desolate and wind-swept until the 20th century. At that time, transportation improved and developers created a middle-class community of small, row houses.

Victorian Homes near Golden Gate Park (right)

Although many grand Victorians were destroyed in the Great Fire of 1906, over 14,000 houses built after the fires continue to grace the city's hills.

Victorian Home Detail (opposite)

San Francisco's signature style, in large part, comes from its numerous, historic Victorian houses. Nearly 48,000 homes were built in this popular style between the gold rush years of the mid-1800s and 1915.

Coit Tower and Christopher Columbus Statue *(above)*

Telegraph Hill was originally a signal tower for ships entering the Golden Gate. A watchman identified ships by their flags and telegraphed the information to Fisherman's Wharf. A plaque in front of the Columbus statue marks the watchman's original spot.

The Rooftop at Yerba Buena Gardens *(oposite)*

The Rooftop is an ambitious development on top of the underground section of the Convention Center that is devoted to children. It features Zeum, a high-tech arts and production center where kids create multimedia art, shows, and video animations.

The Last Doggie *(above)*

When the infamous seven-foot Doggie Diner Sign toppled in a gust of wind, locals were moved to tears. The San Francisco icon was the last of 50 signs for the restaurant chain, popular for its hot dogs in the 1960s and '70s. Now, after an extensive nose job, the 600-lb dachshund lives on 45th Street.

"Cupid's Span" Sculpture *(above)*

"Cupid's Span" is a six-story-high fiberglass sculpture created by international sculptors Claes Oldenburg and Coosje van Bruggen. Rincon Park and this sculpture were a gift to the city by The Gap clothing stores' founders Doris and Donald Fisher, whose world headquarters face the park.

Sunset on Mount Tamalpais, from Tilden Park *(above)*

Just north of San Francisco's Golden Gate is Mount Tamalpais, over 6,000 acres of redwood groves and oak woodlands with a spectacular view from the mountain's 2,571-foot peak.

The Palace of Fine Arts *(opposite)*

Built to celebrate the discovery of the Pacific Ocean and the completion of the Panama Canal, the Palace also celebrated its own resurrection after the shattering earthquake and fire of 1906.

Conservatory of Flowers
(opposite and above)

Opened in 1883, this splendid green-house is modeled after London's famous Palm House in Kew Gardens and is the oldest glass-and-wood Victorian greenhouse in the western hemisphere. Visitors can walk through four different gardens and a separate area for seasonal exhibits.

The Conservatory is home to more than 10,000 plants. Shown above is the "Lowland Tropics," a warm and moist garden filled with beautiful, tropical plants. Other gardens include "Highland Tropics," "Aquatic Plants" and "Victorian Pot Culture."

Orchid *(above)*

Common symbols In different cultures, orchids have represented love, virility, luxury, and beauty. At the Conservatory of Flowers, orchids fascinate visitors because of the fragile complexities of their exotic shapes and colors.

Japanese Tea Garden *(opposite)*

On an average weekend, 75,000 people visit Golden Gate Park. Many come to stroll along the meditative paths amidst ponds, waterfalls, statues, and pagodas. The Garden's teahouse is a wonderful place to relax and enjoy the tranquility of this special place.

Japanese Tea Garden
(above and opposite)

Originally developed as the Japanese Village for San Francisco's 1894 California Midwinter International Exposition, the Tea Garden was designed by landscape gardener Makoto Hagiwara. Appointed caretaker in 1895, he and his family lived in a 17-room house in the Sunken Garden area for 48 years.

Dutch Windmill (opposite)

This restored Dutch Windmill in Golden Gate Park was built in 1902 as a fresh-water pumping station to move underground water to a reservoir on Strawberry Hill. It became obsolete by 1913. At the base of the mill, the Queen Wilhelmina Tulip Garden blossoms each spring.

Ferry Building Clock Tower, The Embarcadero (above)

Originally completed in 1898, the monumental Beaux Arts Ferry Building was the primary point of arrival and departure for San Francisco until the construction of the Golden Gate and Bay Bridges in the late 1930s.

Full Moon on Telegraph Hill
(previous page)

On Telegraph Hill's upper Grant
Avenue, the nearby cafes and shops
still exude Beatnik funkiness. The
scenic boardwalk, Filbert Steps,
meanders down from Coit Tower
through the Grace Marchand
Gardens to Levi's Plaza.

California Academy of Sciences *(top)*

In 1853, just a few years after the
town of Yerba Buena became San
Francisco, the Academy was
founded to survey and study the
vast resources of California and
beyond and specifically the effects
of the Gold Rush. Today, as one of
the 10 largest natural history
museums in the world, the
Academy brings the message of
research to nearly one and a half
million visitors annually.

Asian Art Museum *(left and right)*

The Asian Art Museum exhibits nearly 15,000 treasures from 6,000 years of history from diverse Asian cultures. The collection ranges from tiny jades to monumental sculptures of stone, bronze, wood, and other materials, along with paintings on screens, hanging scrolls and other formats, porcelains and ceramics, lacquers, textiles, furniture, arms and armor, puppets, and basketry. The museum is one of the largest in the Western world devoted exclusively to Asian art.

View from Twin Peaks *(above)*

Market Street appears as a ribbon of lights in this nighttime view from the Twin Peaks. At 49 square miles, San Francisco is really quite small; yet, it has more distinctly defined neighborhoods within its hilly terrain than a city five times its size.

Sunset over San Francisco Bay *(opposite)*

It could have been either 200 years of sloppy navigation or just the fog, but everyone kept missing the Bay. It wasn't until an overland expedition led by Don Gaspar de Portola arrived in 1770 that Europeans came upon the Bay.

Golden Gate Bridge in Fog *(above)*

This is how most people see the Golden Gate Bridge at certain times of the day, but then, the first person chosen to take a symbolic, solitary walk across the bridge on opening day in 1937 never saw it either. She was blind, with her guide dog leading the way.

Marin Headlands in Fog *(opposite)*

Across the Golden Gate Bridge from San Francisco are the spectacular, rocky cliffs of the Marin Headlands. Scenic Cozelman Road will take you to the top to watch the crashing waves below and the breathtaking, panoramic views of the city and the Bay.

Lombard Street *(above)*

Known as the "crookedest street" in San Francisco, surprisingly, it is neither the crookedest nor the steepest. Yet, on any day, you can watch squealing motorists maneuver the street's hairpin turns as they career down this flower-covered hill.

Gathering Storm *(opposite)*

At night, the Golden Gate Bridge may appear to be darker at the top. It is an illusion deliberately created by the bridge's designer. Lighting instructions specified that the bridge towers have less light at the top, so the bridge would seem to soar beyond the range of illumination.

Transamerica Pyramid *(above)*

At first, people were unreceptive to the pyramid-shaped skyscraper. Architect William Pereira claimed that the 853-ft-high building would be a statement of architectural sculpture. Its decorative aluminum spire is the perfect topping to a truly unique city.

Fog and Full Moon *(above)*

Engineer Joseph Strauss designed a rather unsightly suspension structure in 1916. Attempts were made to refine the design, yet it wasn't until consulting architects Irving and Gertrude Morrow stepped in that the current design was finally implemented. The bridge opened for traffic in 1937.

Aerial View of San Francisco *(above)*

The steep gradients in downtown can often make parking danger-ous, but on the plus side—these challenging hills have produced the most powerful fleet of bicycle messengers in the world!

Fairmont Hotel, Nob Hill *(above)*

When this Beaux-arts hotel atop Nob Hill opened its doors soon after the 1906 Great Fire, it was an instant success with the city's elite. Recently renovated, its penthouse continues to be popular with visiting foreign dignitaries and U.S. presidents.

The Bay Bridge at Twilight *(above)*

On March 23, 1872, one of the city's most beloved and eccentric residents, Emperor Norton, ordered the construction of a bridge joining Oakland Point with Yerba Buena Island. The San Francisco-Oakland Bay Bridge didn't become a reality until 1936.

Bank of America Center *(above)*

One of the most recognized buildings in the United States and a focal point of the city's skyline, this 52-story skyscraper was the tallest building west of the Mississippi until it was surpassed by its neighbor, the Transamerica Pyramid, in 1972.

Gateway to Chinatown *(top)*

San Francisco's Chinatown is the greatest single concentration of Chinese people outside of Asia. Eighty-thousand residents live in roughly 24 square blocks, making it the most densely populated area of San Francisco and one of the city's favorite tourist attractions.

Chinatown *(bottom)*

The most exciting time to visit Chinatown is during the celebration of the Chinese New Year, when the narrow streets overflow with a dazzling parade of people in fantastic masks and costumes, and the air is filled with music and fireworks.

Chinese Lanterns *(above)*

More than just decorations in China, paper lanterns have silently communicated births, deaths, social status and approaching danger for over 2,000 years. Red lanterns are popular totems for good luck and long life.

Balclutha Clipper Ship *(above)*

This 1886 square-rigger is one of Aquatic Park's vintage vessels. After sailing the high seas for 44 years, Balclutha is now a popular tourist attraction and a unique setting for special events.

Haight and Ashbury *(opposite)*

Few signs say "flower power" and evoke images of hippies better than this famous San Francisco intersection. Today it is a vibrant, neighborhood with chic boutiques, Internet cafes, and great restaurants.

Ghirardelli Square and Aquatic Park *(above)*

The original factory of famed chocalatier Domingo Ghirardelli is now a lovely brick-terraced court-yard of shops and restaurants adjacent to Aquatic Park's National Maritime Museum and fleet of historic vessels.

Japantown, Geary Boulevard *(oposite)*

This three-story-high stylized white pagoda is a centerpiece for the recently refurbished Peace Plaza in Japantown—the vibrant, bustling home to 12,000 residents of Japanese descent.

Carousel at Pier 39 *(above)*

A short walk from Fisherman's Wharf, Pier 39 is a vibrant shopping and dining area. Visitors enjoy the antics of a colony of sea lions offshore, as well as exhibits in the Pier's Aquarium of the Bay. Few can resist a nostalgic ride on the classic Venetian carousel.

Sausalito Fountain *(opposite)*

Sausalito is a picturesque town across the bay from San Francisco, just north of the Golden Gate Bridge in Marin County. Named by Spanish explorers for its many willow trees, Sausalito covers just two and one-half miles of prime real estate with spectacular waterfront views.

Mission Dolores *(opposite)*

The Mission San Francisco de Asisi, (now Mission Dolores), completed in 1791, is the oldest building in the city.

City Hall *(above)*

Designed by renowned architect Arthur Brown Jr., City Hall opened in 1915. This massive, granite building encompasses two city blocks and is regarded by many to be one of the most important examples of Beaux-arts architecture in the world.

Saint Francis Hotel *(opposite)*

The Saint Francis Hotel in Union Square opened in 1904 and quickly became the center of San Francisco's social, literary, and artistic life. Rebuilt after the 1906 earthquake/fire in its original European-style splendor, this old-world hotel remains at the heart of city life.

Window Shopping *(left)*

Window displays in Union Square boutiques give just a hint of the haute couture treasures inside that await shoppers with labels like Dior, Armani, Marc Jacobs, and Yves Saint Laurent.

Legion of Honor Museum *(right)*

This beautiful Beaux-arts building is a replica of Napoleon's original Legion of Honor building in Paris. The museum's impressive collection spans 4,000 years of ancient and European art in a panoramic setting overlooking the Golden Gate Bridge.

Old Mission Dolores *(left and right)*

The oldest building in San Francisco, Mission Dolores (a.k.a. Mission San Francisco de Asisi) opened its doors in 1776. It miraculously survived the earthquake and fire of 1906 and continues today as the center of spiritual and social life in its community.

Great American Music Hall *(opposite)*

San Francisco's oldest and grandest nightclub opened in 1907 as Blanco's. It soon became the most notorious entertainment spot of the Barbary Coast era, offering prostitution, gambling, booze and food. Renovated in 1972 to showcase its ornate architecture, the new Great American Music Hall has showcased world-famous artists such as Duke Ellington, Sarah Vaughan, Bobby McFerrin, and the Grateful Dead.

Mission Dolores Cemetery *(above)*

Many notable San Franciscans, including the first Mexican governor, are buried in the cemetery of this 230-year-old mission church. It is the oldest surviving building in the San Francisco Bay area. Over 5,000 natives of the Ohlone and Miwok tribes and other First Californians are buried here.

San Francisco National Cemetery, The Presidio *(opposite)*

Originally an Army post cemetery, the Presidio became the first national cemetery on the West Coast in 1884 to provide a final resting place for America's veterans and their families.

Sea Lions at Fisherman's Wharf
(above)

The Pier 39 sea lions took over some of the nearby docks in 1990, and now they are a year-round tourist attraction. People love to watch them bark raucously as they jockey for prime spots in the sun.

The Embarcadero and the Ferry Building (opposite)

After the 1989 San Francisco earthquake, the damaged double-decker freeway was demolished, paving the way for a completely revitalized and unobstructed waterfront centered on the historic Ferry Building.

**Moscone Convention Center
Exhibition Hall** *(top and bottom)*

This great architectural complex is a tribute to George Moscone, the San Francisco mayor who was killed in 1978 by a former member of the city's Board of Supervisors who opposed Moscone's liberal policies. Also killed that day was Harvey Milk, the city's first openly gay supervisor. Moscone was the first mayor to appoint large numbers of minorities to city government positions.

City Hall *(opposite)*

Even as a reflection in a window, City Hall's gold-leaf dome shines brilliantly—the perfect crown for this magnificent Beaux-arts building. The fifth largest dome in the world, it rises 306 feet above ground, a full 14 inches higher than the U.S. Capitol's dome.

Rodin's "Thinker" *(above)*

One of the most famous sculptures in the world, Rodin's Thinker sits in the Legion of Honor Musuem's Court of Honor and is one of 70 Rodin sculptures donated by a single collector. The beautiful Beaux-arts building commemorates 3,600 Californian soldiers who died in World War I.

BART Train *(opposite)*

This section of the Bay Area Rapid Transit system travels down the middle of Highway 24. One look at rush hour traffic can make riding the rails a very attractive alternative.

Neon Lights of Broadway (opposite)

This bustling theater district is San Francisco's answer to Times Square. Theater-goers enjoy a variety of productions including Broadway musicals, classic dramas, and contemporary productions.

Christmas at Union Square (top)

Union Square is a shopper's paradise where major department stores and exclusive coutures are within walking distance. Recently renovated Union Square plaza is a comfortable place to shop or enjoy the talents of street performers, art exhibits, and concerts.

The Castro Movie Theatre (bottom)

An historic landmark, the Castro Theatre is one of the best preserved examples of a 1920s movie palace in the United States. Designed to resemble a Spanish cathedral, it also reinforces the notion of the movie house as a secular cathedral.

The Presidio along Marina Green
(above)

This pristine area just south of the Golden Gate was established in 1776, marking the beginning of 211 years of rule by Spain, then Mexico and, eventually, the United States. Today the Presidio is a living museum of history with more than 500 historic buildings, coastal defense fortifications, a national cemetery, and an historic airfield. The history lesson is enhanced with spectacular vistas, forests, marshes, and beaches. Adjacent to the Presidio is Marina Green, popular for jogging, kite-flying, sunbathing and picnicking.

**Architectural Detail,
City Hall Historic Landmark** *(above)*

Exquisite architectural details, such as this decorative female figure, are the reasons why City Hall is known as "the Crown Jewel" of the finest ensemble of classical architecture in America.

Point Bonita Lighthouse *(opposite)*

Originally built in 1855 on a higher location on the northern tip of the Golden Gate, the Point Bonita Lighthouse was so high above the water that it was usually shrouded in fog and virtually useless to mariners. Today it continues to transmit a steady beacon from its original 150-year-old lens.

Rainbow at Rodeo Beach *(above)*

There is a real national treasure at the end of this rainbow, and you can get to it on a city bus! Rodeo Beach, located in the Marin Headlands, is rich in wildlife, flora and dramatic geology. Migrating birds use the lagoon as one of their stops along the way.

Sutro Tower on Twin Peaks *(above)*

High atop Mount Sutro, Sutro Tower rises up another nearly 1000 feet, transmitting television and radio signals to the surrounding communities. Twin Peaks is a popular climb through eucalyptus forests that rewards hikers with stunning, panoramic views.

The Historic Ferry Building *(opposite)*

San Francisco Chronicle columnist Herb Caen once wrote, "The waterfront without the Ferry Tower would be like a birthday cake without a candle." A waterfront icon since 1898, the historic building is now renovated and hosts a mix of office space, shops, and restaurants.

Jogger at Crissy Fields
(above)

Once a rich, salt marsh, Crissy Fields has been transformed into a 100-acre park. It features a waterfront promenade, revitalized native sand dunes, an expanded beach, and scenic outlooks.

Sunset on the Golden Gate Bridge
(opposite)

The Golden Gate Bridge is a fitting symbol of San Francisco's inexhaustible spirit. Many critics said it was simply crazy to try to build a bridge across such a wide and dangerous bay. Yet here it stands, soaring and gleaming in its bright, vermillion paint. This engineering marvel has helped bring a center and wholeness to the communities of San Francisco Bay, and it has proven to the world that anything is possible in San Francisco.

Brad Perks

Brad Perks lives in the San Francisco Bay Area. He has spent a lifetime taking pictures of California and the Western States. Perks started his professional career photographing events for Levis, the GAP and the San Francisco Ballet. Perks has also been hired to photograph such notable people as Vice President Quayle, Patrick Swayze, Isabella Rossellini, Ester Williams and Joe DiMaggio.

Perks was selected as the official Bay Area photographer for the Millennium Photo Project in 1999. 2000 photographers from around the world had 24 hours to photograph the turn of the Millennium. Fireworks over San Francisco went on to win an international award.

Perks now devotes his full attention to photographing scenic landscapes. His award winning images are published around the world. His clients include the Sierra Club, San Francisco Magazine, Shutterbug, Twin Lights Publishers, Hewlett Packard, Redwood National Park and Bay Nature Magazine. Perks favorite quote is from Ansel Adams: "Sometimes I arrive just when God's ready to have someone click the shutter."

Brad Perks pictures are available as commercial Stock Photography and Limited Edition Prints. They can be seen on the web at PC Image Network and Lightscapes Photo Gallery, pcimagenetwork.com.